INTUITIVE POEMS FOR A JOYFUL AND WOUNDED HEART

INTUITIVE POEMS FOR A

JOYFUL
AND
WOUNDED
HEART

Spignotta E. Milam

Intuitive Poems for a Joyful and Wounded Heart

Published in the United States, Intuitive Thoughts Publishing Company

Email: Spignotta59@Yahoo.com

First Edition
ISBN: 979-8-9872934-0-9

TABLE OF CONTENTS

This book of Intuitive Poems was written over a time span of 14 years.

To help you as the reader have a clear meaning of intuitive poetry, I'll give you my definition:

Intuition is the preconceived thought regarding an action or event. It is equivalent to looking into the future with a spiritual eye and giving justification and clarity to a thought, action or deed.

Several of these poems have been used in a therapeutic environment to help clients express emotions, thoughts and feelings regarding a particular crisis or celebration occurring within their lives at that time.

Spiritual Perspectives

Sometimes we're so used to adversity that when we have commitments or life-changing responsibilities, we like swallow our pain so that we can step up to whatever task or duty is needed to be done at that time. And then one day, we are so full, we crack. There is no more space for us *not* to address our pain.

The spiritual side of you is the ammunition needed to help keep you from staying cracked and totally getting off track and risking not fulfilling your purpose. The spiritual side of you encourages you, providing hope and inner knowing that things will get better, with faith as a prescription to help you persevere.

PRAYER

Today as I wait in anticipation, hoping against strife,

Hoping against another message of rejection,

I remember that no matter the answer to the initial question,

You are the final answer to my everyday existence.

You are my triumphs and soothe me when my analysis tells me I have failed.

As long as you stay with me and keep me focused, there can be no bad days—

Only lessons to learn for the next day.

Amen.

ANXIETY

Today the stress is compounding.

Today the sweat is pouring from my brow as I try to keep from hyperventilating from the challenges that face me.

Today as the phone rings nonstop with another dramatic message of

"I need you to take care of this now,"

I remember the answer to all unanswered questions is you, GOD.

For you are the author and finisher of all things.

I remember that you can change the impossible to possible.

I remember that it is only a test, not the final outcome of if I am doing a good job in your eyesight.

For you have that all-seeing Eye.

You penetrate inside the depths of my soul, heart, mind, body and being.

I have an eye. You are the one who makes the "I."

So today, as stuff hits the fan and the pan, I can relax knowing you got my back, front, my sides, my top and my bottom.

You regulate the regulator.

Thank you for reminding me that stress is the devil's tool to steal the joy you promised me.

If I believe in you and your word, everything will be within my grasp and you will not withhold any good thing from me.

A PRAYER OF THANKSGIVING AND RENEWED DIRECTION

Today I reflect on the multiplicity of GOD's blessings within my life's circle.

I thank you, God, especially for renewed life.

I thank you for true friends, true confidants and renewed strength.

I thank you for a renewed mind and continued change in perspective.

I thank you for the prayer warriors, seen and unseen.

I thank you for constantly bringing situations and troubled people into my horizon for me to minister to so I won't focus so much time on my minute shortcomings that you have already addressed.

I thank you for the challenges that you put before me that remind me that it's my faith and trust in you that has brought me this far, not man's accolades and paycheck.

I thank you for allowing me to feel great and healthy.

I thank you for constantly enlarging my territory and my mission.

I ask you now to open the minds of my seed and the new seeds that you have entrusted in my care. Give them a sense of your purpose for them.

Give them a sense of direction to reach their goal. Give them a voice of discernment so they will know what path to take toward fulfillment of their purpose.

Give me a renewed heart and willing mind to serve
your children that you have entrusted to me. Give me
a renewed desire and expanded vision to continue
to think outside the box, by any means necessary,
to save your lost sheep. Give me parents willing to
think outside the box that will change their
perspectives to benefit their children.

Give me the renewed strength to multitask and outlast
the stumbling blocks and negativity placed before me.

Thank you for making my Dreams and visions materialize.
Thank you for allowing me occasional physical release.

Thank you for all these and the multitude of blessings
past, present and future, too numerous to recall and too
numerous to know.

In Jesus' name, I pray this prayer of Thanksgiving.

Amen.

BUS PROPHET

You can find wisdom in the strangest places. Especially when you aren't looking for it.

When we are of calm demeanor and have an open mind, God can manifest in the most unlikely places.

He can use whom he chooses to spit us a word of Gospel pearls that redirects and objects to our current mode of thought,

Yet captures our heart and sense of judgment till we have to adhere to the wisdom moment and alter our thought. Today as I was on my way, I came upon such a man.

A Bus Prophet, you understand, spitting truth after truth, shouting to the roof the knowledge he must expel, no matter, pray tell, the cost.

Because the Boss of all had given him a mission, a calling to fulfill.

Bus Prophet, thank you for reminding me it isn't the outer self but the inner self.

It's not the type of transportation we use to get there, but that we reach our destination no matter what.

FORGIVENESS

Today, my Lord, I come to you asking for forgiveness. For all the times l made him the center of my universe.

Please forgive me for putting so much energy and time into one man, who was not you.

Today, Lord, I thank you for giving me the gift of Repentance. For you could have struck me down so long ago for putting another person before you.

Thank you for your mercy.

Thank you for being so good to me.

FRIENDSHIP

As I ponder our dilemma, I remember that we are
truly blessed.

Because we have true friendship.

A friendship that meets the needs of the two of us.

A friendship of give-and-take.

A friendship of honesty and commitment.

To be friends no matter what.

A friendship that seeks to build and grow.

A friendship that seeks the unanswered

And is not content with just letting things be.

A friendship that meets the other where they are,

As opposed to where you want them to be.

A friendship that supports and doesn't abandon when the
script changes or a new issue is presented contrary to one
or the other.

Friendship can be a trip sometimes.

Thank God our Friendship has truly been a great adventure.

GOD IS WORKING BEHIND THE SCENES

God is working behind the scenes.

God is working behind the scenes cleaning up messes we caused here and there and in between.

Almighty God is working behind the scenes.

You take one step, God takes two. Whatever is necessary to pull you through.

Today I profess and can attest,

My God is working behind the scenes.

Challenges come in multiplicity. Challenges that test your resolve and someday try to make you question your divinity.

But just remember one thing that always holds true: our mighty God will never desert you.

Some days you might not feel him. Some days you might not be able to see Him, and there are times when you don't hear Him.

But God is always working behind the scenes.

INDULGENCE IN HIS LOVE

Indulgence and emergence in the warmth and the comfort of God's goodness and mercy.

Indulge in the fulfillment of His Scriptures that state, "God is Love."

Indulge in the safety of His arms that will never let you go.

JESUS, JESUS

Jesus, feed my soul.
Jesus, make me whole.
Jesus is my anchor, my sunshine, my comforter.
Jesus, you are my all in all.

JOY

GOD, it is a joy to wake up and receive your road map
for this day. It is a blessing to realize how blessed
we really are.

GOD, you protect us from the seen and unseen dangers.

You protect us from ourselves.

Only God knows how many times I was tempted to do
wrong, and God provided a detour to keep me on the
straight and narrow road of righteousness.

Joy—the excited feeling we have when we know we have
dodged a bullet.

God, thank you for showing up every day.

You are our Father.

Thank you, God, for showing up when no one else will.

Thank you for being the final answer and solution to
every crisis.

LORD, GIVE US A WORD

Lord, give me the words because my words to express the anger and fears within me are not Godly words.

I told you it would be alright if you changed my name.

Now that my name has been changed, and my mind has been changed, give me new powerful words to propel me into my destiny.

Let me not speak words that will delay, or convey, that I am not one of your children.

Don't let my anger speak words that will block my blessings.

Lord, give me a word, a holy word.

A word to empower, lift up and release hope instead of hopelessness.

Lord, give me a word that edifies you, not denies you.

Thank you for the words of Jesus.

For they have not only increased my vocabulary, but have increased the joy in my soul.

MISSIONARY'S PRAYER

Agape Love is unconditional, unbreakable love, which is known as affection without limitations. It is Love without conditions, and above all, it is Love that is patient and not envious, rude or quick to take offense.

Let each one whom the services are meant for awaken their spirit of curiosity and thirst to know more and seek more about you, LORD JESUS.

Lord, as we go out into this worldly vineyard to preach, teach and nurture your Word through actions and words that exhibit service and servitude to your higher calling,

Let not our actions, words and deeds, done in the name of JESUS, fall on unfertile ground.

Let our works as missionaries lead and unite others to be a part of your Army of Glory.

As we travel to unchartered territories where no witnesses to your Word have ever been before, allow your Grace and Mercy to meet us there. Give us words, wisdom and understanding to reach new disciples in Jesus' name.

As a missionary, you must practice Agape Love daily in your mission to reach others through spreading the Gospel of JESUS CHRIST.

You must witness Love, GOD's gift to us.

MONEY CAN'T BUY YOU

Money can't buy you happiness. Money can't buy you Love.

Money can create a better environment, like the ones you have been dreaming of.

Money can help establish you.

Character is the substance that sustains you.

Money can't buy you happiness. Money can't buy you Love. Having money will ease your pain but won't eliminate it.

Having money will give you access to the world of materialism,

But not increase your Spiritualism.

MONEY CAN'T BUY YOU HAPPINESS OR LOVE.

MY AWAKENING

My soul speaks to change. Change in circumstance, in location, in occupation, and new change in the primary focus on my life.

No longer chasing your dreams and putting mine on the back burner.

Learning a new level of patience. Learning to embrace waiting on God.

Learning that change makes you depend on God more because it takes you out of your comfort zone.

Working on, leaning on, building on, tuning into God's voice in my heart as the navigator. My soul has embraced this change. My heart welcomes this change.

Now I must practice due diligence as God's plan unfolds for me.

I can't get distracted by the noise of the past or the drama of the present, which acts as a filter to make me continue to lean in and not seek the counsel of the unwise.

God has removed me from my physical support system of friends.

He has taken my carnal livelihood away. He has placed me in an environment where my chief duty is to pray and anoint.

I must wait on Him to give me my next assignment in His own appointed time.

As Scripture states: But they that wait upon the Lord shall renew their strength; they shall mount up with wings as eagles.

(Isaiah 40:31, KJV).

Well, my soul awaits your instruction and road map as I venture into this new dimension of happiness.

Thank you for this new level of peace and tranquility. In Jesus Christ, I pray, Amen.

NEW LEVELS, NEW DEVILS

GOD is in the blessing business.

We have the everyday blessing of life itself. We have those finite blessings that the only limitation is the scope of our vision, or perception of what God will bless us with.

We have those blessings that are so monumental that the world, as well as ourselves, knows it's a supernatural reward that only God can manifest.

Our level of blessings has so much to do with how we receive it.

Do we acknowledge and thank God for the small things and for everything in our lives?

Do we understand that the more God blesses us, the more haters and jealous people around us become?

Are you strong enough to be thankful for your blessing, in spite of losing the favor of man?

Man, whom you thought would rejoice instead of renounce you for your good fortune.

Just remember that with every new level God takes you to, there's a new devil waiting to desecrate instead of elevate your praise to the most high God.

PAIN & SHAME MET ME AT THE CROSS

They came to war with me as I laid my burdens down.

My past and the forecast for my future laid down.

They came to convince me of my unworthiness to be saved.

But I adhered to the Word: "Come unto me, all ye that labour and are heavy laden, and I will give you rest."

(Matthew 11:28, KJV)

I embraced the pain and released them at the cross.

The past stood before me, yet Jesus still adored me.

He forgave all my transgressions.

Now the pain and shame of yesterday fled.

Now I'm a new creature who released it all at the cross.

I claim Jesus as my Savior.

Yes, now I claim Jesus as my Savior and Lord.

The holy story I've become.

I've exchanged my pain and shame for the love of God.

PANDEMIC RESPONSE

Children are stressed, though they are blessed to live in an environment that meets their basic needs. Parents are overwhelmed by the reality of learning and realizing how much they do not control. They are now faced with the reality of the only way they have control is how they choose to respond to having no control. For the first time in a long time, parents are forced to parent their child. Nobody wants to babysit unruly children when it's not a pandemic. During a pandemic, nobody wants to babysit at all. All of your usual coping adventures have become cautious exercises that require more personal protection equipment (PPE), such as double masking up, face shield, taking Airborne to go to events where there are large crowds in enclosed areas, where you are only a chair apart indoors.

Yet for those who have always known GOD is in control, we focus on the blessings instead of the challenges. We mask up, sanitize, and critically decide where we must go and where we do not have to go for safety protocols. Yet we marvel at all the people we thought were smart and well balanced but who remain unvaccinated and unconcerned about how their selfishness can harm loved ones in danger as carriers of this commutable disease. We as soldiers of Christ and believers of justice for all people, we now find ourselves praying more and spending time with the blockheads only when we have to. We advocate peace even though we know in America, agitation is the primary instrument of change. More and more, kindness is seen as weakness and bullying as an attribute. We now have new awareness for a need to pray for your enemies. Because until people conform and adapt to a philosophy that we must care for one another whether we like them or not, we are all destined to die due to their foolishness. Even if we only pray and ask GOD to change their hearts and minds by giving them a loving spirit to replace the self-centered, greedy mindset. Thank you for being a truly caring, productive individual who has refused to alter their purpose due to fear and the new added challenges to do so.

PERSEVERANCE

News each day is depressing. Weather alerts with rising heat indexes. All these alarming details are constantly bombarding us. We have to rely on what we can trust. Trust in GOD. Trust your Instincts. Trust that the Pandemic reminds us how little control we have.

That is why spiritual reconnection like Ephesians 6:11 KJV, which states, "Put on the whole armor of God," is so important. So today, give the world your brightest smile. Mask up, pray up, get up and recognize God is in control and put your faith in Him, knowing your breakthrough is dawning.

PREPARATION FOR CHANGE

The sun is shining bright and illuminating the room with radiant sunlight. The leaves on the trees are stilled by the lack of wind. The birds are gathering in their migratory formation headed to their annual family reunion on the southern border. Squirrels scurry to pick up nuts to complete their nature shopping list ahead of the winter. They sense a forthcoming of the change in season. The early mornings dawn with lower temperatures. Meteorologists forecast shorter days with high temps and more days with low temps. The wind periodically makes its blistery presence known. This is a precursor to ice-cutting turbulence to come, just around the corner.

Trees that were once covered with full plumages of green leaves and vibrant flowers now have transcended to that Fall hue from green to burnt orange and yellow. The flowers are now dying and falling off the tree to fertilize the ground for the upcoming Spring thaw.

Human bodies are adjusting to the cooler temperatures and increasing the layers of clothing in anticipation of the onslaught of winter. Oil changes, tire checks and adding ice scrapers to the interior of the car are a new necessity. In your trunk you have put a blanket, bag of cat litter, shovel, jumper cables and flashlight. Visits to the grocery store include adding hot chocolate packets, soup, crackers and ingredients for pot stew or gumbo. These are the entrées you crave on a cold, blistery day. It is so beautiful yet subtle how God has all his creatures perform in a gradual transition from one season to the next. We all subconsciously slowly adapt to the inevitable shift of the season. Thank God for reminding us that change is inevitable and always forthcoming. We must learn to be better prepared for it is surely coming as we need air to breathe.

PROMISE FULFILLED

You promised me that when I accepted you as my Lord and Savior, you would never forsake me.

You promised me you would be there during the darkness of my existence.

You promised you would be there when all around me was trouble and defeat.

You were answered prayer when my back was against the wall and all exits to a better reality were closed shut.

No human was equipped or available to handle the problem.

Only you, GOD, came through.

When doctors said hospice was the next step, you said Jesus was the only step.

When my boss said you are fired, you said, now it's time to create the job you wanted to do all along.

When your mate procrastinates and forgets to put in the paperwork to secure the dream house God promised you both, instead of feeling defeated, God reminds you he owns it all.

When patience grows thin, waiting against hope and man's time table,

God, you remind us you made man and can eliminate and extend any time table as you see fit.

God, you promised you would be my all in all if I sought you above all other things in my life.

Thank you for fulfilling your promise.

THANKFUL

Thankful for my magnanimous blessings.

Thankful for healthy family members.

Thankful for being healthy and clothed in my right mind.

Thankful for an abundance of resources.

Thankful for the ability to listen to God and follow His instructions.

Thankful God is reuniting my family.

Thankful for a job I enjoy.

Thankful for this season of peace in the midst of a Pandemic.

Thankful for others commending me and recognizing my worth.

Thankful for an abundance of options for the future.

Thankful for constant confirmation that I am a child of God.

He will not leave me or forsake me.

Thankful for reaping the benefits from past generational prayers.

Thankful for being taught how to pray and how to listen to God's voice speaking.

I am honored to be your servant, Lord.

REFLECTION

The wisdom of our elders whom we see every day is taken for granted until they are suddenly taken away.

Father, Son and Holy Ghost, all are of importance; who is to say which one you need most.

The elder spokesperson has now passed on. He is gone to another place beyond our reach. He is now calling on us to have instant recall of all the lessons of which he preached.

We are to use his lifelong lessons as a script of what to avoid and what to embrace, knowing no one can ever take his place.

We are asking and receiving strength to carry on.

Asking for guidance that the life I lead will show itself as a living testament that I am the character embodiment of fruit from his seed.

So this day, I say farewell to my elder example of manhood and masculinity.

I thank you for the lessons you taught and the lessons we learned together.

I now wish you Godspeed on your next assignment.

TRIBUTE TO THOSE GONE ON...

God in his infinite wisdom puts families together.

Today we celebrate the unique personalities and cherished family members' lives whose physical presence is no longer with us.

We celebrate each and every one of our deceased family members' contributions to the glue that continues to hold this family together.

We celebrate their birth, their laughter, the challenges they endured to make us better persons, as well as how those challenges helped them grow, and flourish, within our family.

We celebrate the continuance of their existence in our hearts and minds through the lessons they taught us and the triumphant way they help bring us through, to this place where we are now, as a family.

We ask that the spirits of our ancestors and the deep Christian principles they shared with us continue to sustain and prosper all of the members of this family.

And may we be a testament to the lives that they lived and the life we are living now.

Let us not take God's grace for granted. Let us not take each other for granted.

Let us continue to hold these reunions as a source of strengthening family values and family history.

For you can't know where you're going if you don't know where you have been.

God in his infinite wisdom has made us family and lets us continue to strengthen and not divide, encourage and not discourage, and help and not hinder others who look to us as the elders and voices of wisdom within this family.

Let the spirit of all those who have gone from us become a bright light of hope in the midst of the despair that happens in the course of living. And let our living never be in vain.

Thank you for all you have taught us.

Thank you for how far you have brought us.

Thank you for instilling in us the connective unity of family, now and forever. Amen.

WHAT CAN I SAY?

What can I say after a day like today?

God has cosigned the desires of my heart.

God has blessed me with friends who show they care,
not just say they care. God has blessed me with
comforters I can touch, not just feel. And comforters
who fill me up with their air of positive energy
and goodwill blessings.

What Can I Say? Tomorrow promises to be even
better than today with limitless opportunities
for greatness.

What Can I Say, but after a month, week, day like today,
the only thing left to say is, What Can I Say?

YOU ARE LOVED

You are loved. You are valued.

You have purpose.

You are uniquely and beautifully made.

Hand-sculpted by GOD, the all-powerful.

How does mere man's perception of you hold more weight than GOD?

You were created to be man's helpmate.

Meaning you are the greater skilled craftswoman to show up and finish the job when his vision is blurred or at a standstill.

Trials make us stronger emotionally even when we appear beaten physically.

The holy spirit of GOD can renew it all.

CHURCH ON SUNDAY IS GOOD

Church on Sunday is good.

Praying with family is a must.

But how many people can you trust?

How many people do you treat with a Christ-like love?

Do you always turn the other cheek?

Do you aim first and ask questions later?

Are you so on the defense, no love or compassion for a
misunderstanding can penetrate?

Are you always putting down instead of lifting up?

How many angry people have you confused today with
your smile and sunny disposition?

How many hostile angry children have you comforted?

How many hungry people have you fed?

How many naked people have you clothed?

How many wounded hearts have you mended?

How many sick people have you nourished back to health?

How many mentally depressed people have you given hope?

As I said, Church on Sunday is good.

But can you walk the talk, or are you just one of those
one-day Christians who talk the talk out of both sides of
your mouth?

Resilience

In spite of all the things that should have damaged, taken me out, propelled me to being a hard, evil, vindictive woman, I assessed each hurt on an individual basis instead of lumping all the people and situations in the same pot so that my heart and mind would continue to be open to what was healthy or not. I did not allow each new encounter to have to pay the price for the last negative encounter.

So, it has taken resilience to be able to allow each new person their space for me to get to know them and allow them to present themselves instead of me looking to the bad initially.

ARISE

Arise from the ashes of despair.

Arise from the pity party of your existence.

Arise from the broken heart that comes from a
dream unfulfilled.

ARISE.

Arise, get up, get down on your knees and pray
your way out of the hellacious circumstance of
your present state.

Focus on the light permeating from your soul.

It reminds you to be grateful for having the mental
capacity to be able to assess how far you have come.

Now, you need to know where you need to go.

With prayer and thanksgiving for the past, present and
future blessings as you step forward, each day will be
brighter than the day before.

ARISE.

STATE OF MIND

Today you feel confused, misused and abused by your own actions, thoughts and deeds.

Today your knees are almost bleeding from your prayers and cries and pleas.

Today you have grown battle weary, wondering why the answer that should be so simple is so elusive.

Today desperation has become your best friend.

It is crowding out others who love you and stick by you until the bitter end.

What's this malady that is gripping me from within?

Its name is depression, my friend.

It will alter your stride, change your insides and, last but not least, strip you of your pride.

Until one day, you look in the mirror. You see your clothing is disheveled.

Your face has stubble.

You see your whole world is in trouble.

Without knowing the date or time, you have witnessed a change in your State of Mind.

FOOT WARMER

There you are showing that you truly leave no stone unturned.

There you are cradling the baby, as you remove it from his mother's breast and taking the Babe from the slave quarters to where you and your mistress rest.

Not to comfort the Babe, but to comfort you.

You lay him not yet two years old across your feet.

His purpose is to keep you and your lady warm while you sleep.

If you kick him during the night, what do you care?

He is just a slave Babe you are using while he is there.

Foot Warmer, that's his job.

Thrust into servitude as soon as he can walk.

Heaven forbid if he starts to talk.

For silence is Golden and the rule of the day.

For children were to be seen and not heard.

A Foot Warmer, that's the job for toddler slaves.

No time to be nurtured, no time for his mother to hold him and cuddle him in her arms.

This poem is dedicated to my Grandfather - Papa Dennis Williamson, who was born a slave and whose first job was a Foot Warmer for his father, the plantation owner.

LIFE

Life, today, tomorrow, yesterday, life.

Not any life—my life. Boy, life for me ain't been no crystal stair. However, if I had made different choices, who knows where my life would have taken me.

Began my teenage life hangin' out with the boys.

Traded toys for joys of sex and little wine. Then escalated to a dime bag every now and then. Went from a dime, always skirted doing time, to an ounce and hit big time copping a quarter pound.

Didn't want it to sell; wanted it, pray tell, whenever I felt the need to quench my thirst for mother nature's cure with the herb that gives me the munchies and decreases the hunger for your love.

Life, boy, I've had my strife, but being realistic, mine was self-induced.

Couldn't get loose of this Addiction.

It has become an Affliction that turned the statement, "Just try it one more time," into making me a Lifer.

You know I've been puffing and huffing for Joints what to most black men represent a lifetime during these times of Black Male Genocide.

Yes, that's my Life, self-induced strife.

Seeking the high Life as in my next high.

My how time goes by when you lead your Life without a plan.

OVERWHELMED

Rushing in, others, not your direct supervisor, feel compelled to change, alter and add to your job description in a millisecond and expect instantaneous compliance.

Overwhelmed! Task no one else will do; you feel compelled to volunteer…

Overwhelmed by the sheer need of community service.

Home life is a blast. Love ones in your past are fading fast. Parents are getting sick and needing extra hands to recuperate.

Friends call, dumping all their excessive issues. They just want you to commiserate with them on a bummed-out day. Overwhelmed!

Past conflicts, scheduled to be resolved but have been put on the back burner, resurface…crying out for attention like a five-alarm fire.

Your body is craving a love jones, and nobody is home to fulfill the need. Overwhelmed!

Paperwork and bills stacked sky high demanding to be tackled.

All this comes rushing in screaming, shouting to be addressed—now.

Your body reacts in a swell as tension mounts.

Your palms feel sweaty, your temples throb, and your vision blurs under the strain.

Aleve can't even perceive how to take the top off the pain that is playing a refrain in your head.

All this in a 24-hour day! Overwhelmed, I would say.

INTUITIVE LOOK

Slowly I looked inside myself and witnessed all the incomplete parts and disheveled visions of my being. I could clearly see how much I was literally hanging by the tiny threads of hope, anguish and fervent prayers of others throughout the universe who have received random thoughts concerning me needing an extra prayer.

Some of these spirits are newly transitioned into an existence no longer like mine. Others are still here with me awaiting the fulfillment of dreams and harsh realities that remind us of how little we control our world. This new revelation is a strong reminder of the weakness of procrastination. For we never know how much time we truly have to complete the task at hand. We should stay ready as opposed to get ready.

Enjoy each moment instead of dwelling on the fallacy of all the challenges of which we have no control. We should pray daily to anchor our soul. We must respond daily to our GOD-given purpose and complete steps toward fulfilling it daily.

Slowly I turned from inside myself to outside myself and vowed to work on doing my part to spread joy, peace and reconciliation among my brothers and sisters.

I must work to be purpose filled, not bitterly driven by the daggers and pain that constantly pursue us daily.

I also vowed to take time to exhale and process the blessings and stumbling blocks each day brings to the surface. And remember to thank GOD for the blessings of being alive and able to feel pain, sorrow and joy, which are a sharp reminder that we are still here.

FUN

Feeling Iike I need a release from woes and problems.

Understanding that doing something I enjoy will bring me Joy.

Now that's what I call a prescription for FUN.

GOOD FRIENDS

Good friends are like fine wine that has aged to
perfection.

And when you partake of it, the joy excites your
taste buds

And cools your throat muscles as it eases throughout
your entire body.

It gives you a light-headed exuberance of relaxation,
calmness and harmony.

If I was asked to describe what you being a part of my
life means to me,

It would be like drinking the wine of perfection.

It would be like finding your lost family member.

I thank God for bringing you into my life as a companion,
friend and confidant.

As we participate in the mundane task necessary to
operate fulfilling our purpose,

Let us not forget what is really important,

Which is all the lives we have changed for the better
operating in our purpose.

This is where God has stationed us, right now for such a
time as this.

DARRAH'S SONG

Darrah's Song, so tall and strong.

My only regret is she never knew how truly beautiful she was.

The body art was just a part of her individual expression.

It was an added dimension of her creation of what being beautiful was to her. She so did not need it.

Darrah was a beautiful vision of a strong, powerful, black female.

Darrah was stubborn, dedicated and loyal.

Unfortunately, she did not always choose wisely whom to be loyal to.

Darrah, your smile, your spunk, your capacity to captivate will not be lost.

We will remember You!

You will be the voice that reminds me to never give up.

Darrah, your song is not gone.

For there are many lessons we learned through knowing Darrah.

Lesson 1: Listen to your children. "Don't be so judgmental."

Lesson 2: Try to always say something positive when you talk to your child.

Lesson 3: A smile is the beginning tool to soften the most angry of hearts.

Lesson 4: Honesty is the best policy, but you have to also be responsible for the consequences of your actions.

These lessons will help us to grow in the future.

Darrah's Song will truly linger long after the services of the day. For to me, Darrah made an impact.

Her spirit of youthfulness and vitality will be here to encourage us to never give up even when the odds are against us.

For truth will come forward in the end.

GOOD MORNING, MY SISTAH

Today you are at the finish line. Smile and focus on the weekend.

Focus on the sun setting, the heat wave evaporating, and you get to ease your tired muscles with a lap in the pool. You get to wind down from your day with a cool, chilled glass of wine and listen to the melodies of the down-home blues serenading you to relaxation heaven.

Because today, when you get off, "It will be the weekend for you."

Love you.

HOLD FAST TO YOUR DREAMS

Hold fast to your dreams. If you can conceive it and believe it in your mind's eye, it is possible for it to be.

Hold fast to your dreams and remember that it is darkest yet before a breakthrough. So, the more it looks like it's not happening, the closer it actually is to a breakthrough.

GOD sometimes tests our faith just to see how much we want things before He gives them to us.

Hold fast to your dreams and know that all things are possible to him that believes.

Remember that you are always just a prayer away from me.

Remember that communication with GOD involves just an honest one-on-one conversation.

Hold fast to your dreams and know family is not always those who are connected through the womb.

Family can be people who have a connection to your spirit or through your soul.

I thank GOD our paths crossed, for you have challenged me like only a few have in my lifetime. But please hold fast to your dreams.

Keep in touch so, as your dreams are realized, I can witness them with you.

Hold fast to your dreams, and above all things, know that you are loved.

I SEE MYSELF AS A MAN

I see myself as a man striving to be the best man I can be,
facing my demons one by one. I'm working hard to
meet my goals long after the day is done.
I'm trying to right my wrongs.

By making honesty and integrity my path to
righteousness. Staying on my knees begging. Lord,
please let my left turns turn out right.

And make my crooked ones straight. I'm too old to
keep making the same mistakes.

Help me to accept the blessings you place before me.
Restore my confidence and restore my family. Make the
visions in my heart come to the surface.

Let me not be the king of procrastination, but the
servant of service.

Let me embrace my queen and we become one as we
work together to accomplish much.

In Jesus Christ, I pray. Let my seed embrace Thee,

Vision of accomplishment and success. And follow the
path of doing great works. Let my visions become reality
and be a part of a united family. Amen.

LOCKED UP BUT NOT CONFINED

Locked up but not confined.

Being confined with boundaries all around you
is a state of mind.

Like when a person is high, they can see colors that
only exist in a "high" state of reality.

When you write your plan and focus on the reality you
want it to be, instead of the reality it be,

That is when you start to see that your imagination
is endless and you have the ability to think things
into existence.

I'm locked up but not shackled. I'm locked up
but not bridled.

I can express my thoughts and feelings in the dark
window of my mind.

I'm locked up not confined.

I'm locked up but not bound by others' limited
perception of my potential.

I'm locked up but not confined. For confinement
is a state of mind.

SPRUNG FROM THE LOINS OF KINGS

Hey you, Sprung from the Loins of Kings,

Why are you so uptight and acting like you in a fright
about a mere individual when you have GOD on
your side?

Hey you, Sprung from the Loins of Kings,

What is life if not new challenges and new opportunities
to be a living Testament to how GOD will intervene
and cause your troubled waters to appear fresh and
serene when he initiates order on the scene?
Just drop to your knees.

Saying, Father, would you please show me how to
hear your Will clearly? Please direct my actions,
words, thoughts and deeds. Let me not supersede
your Will and forget who is really in charge
of it all.

Let me not forget to thank you for the multitude of
blessings within my Life that occur daily in the midst
of this drama and petty mind-game saga that is
causing me to be frustrated and unhappy in my
own castle of which you, in your infinite Wisdom,
made me large and in charge of this
particular domain.

Hey You, Sprung from the Loins of Kings,

Remember with prosperity comes strife. Remember
with challenges comes the awareness that this is a
part of Life, and without challenges, strife and drama,
we are deceased.

So hold your head up high and don't let your
crown falter.

Stand erect, and bold, and utilize the power you hold.

Be bold, and know that as every door closes,
another opens with blessings you don't have
room enough to receive. Believe it,
for that's Scripture!!!

HOW WILL I KNOW?

How will I know when enough is enough?

How will I know when "we" are ready to commit to life,
to love, 'til death do us part?

How will I know that you are enough for me?

So much enough for me that I give up the right to better
my options forever.

How will I know that this love is strong enough to battle
the seen and unforeseen adversities awaiting us because
we desire to build a life together?

How will I know if my love, dedication and one-track
mindedness at satisfying and tantalizing the love of my life
will be returned or at least, at a minimum, appreciated?

How will I know I won't have the option to put my life on
hold and be cautious just 'til I can be sure?

That is not living. I do know I want to live, love and
experience the joy of being inside you and with you on
whatever terms while I can.

And the "How will I know?" will take care of itself.

SOMEWHERE

Somewhere out there he resides, waiting, longing
for my love besides.

Somewhere out there he must be.

Somewhere out there he is searching for me.

Somewhere out there I know is the man I'm looking for.

I don't want to become discouraged or turn into a
vindictive woman.

I just want to be loved, respected and comforted;
when we meet, he will know which.

Somewhere out there we will meet.

Lord, grant me the patience needed to hold my
peace and wait on his coming.

BABY BLESSINGS

Folks keep forgetting that God's got a sense of humor.

Folks keep forgetting that it's God that's running it and us that is running around in it.

We constantly forget that we put our hands in a man who stilled the waters.

Yet when actions contrary to our proposed life script creep in and give us a trip-up, or a slipup, on our flight plan,

We sometimes forget that all blessings aren't immediately obvious.

Some are shrouded in controversy. Others appear to come out of thin air.

Like when your baby comes home with those big beautiful eyes and smile, saying, I love you.

You had such high expectations of me. I don't want to let you down.

But I've just encountered my first speed bump.

In a few months, you will become a grandparent...

While you bask in the shock of the news of expectancy, remember first the privilege and the blessing bestowed upon her as the carrier of this seed.

MY ELDEST BROTHER

Everyone who has ever had an older sibling remembers a time when you did not agree.

Well, me and my big brother were 12 years apart in age.

He really felt like he could tell me what to do and it be undisputed.

As a child growing up during hard times and good times, my Big Brother was larger than life.

He was the official man of the house.

He worked jobs after school so we would have the things we needed.

He bought Dani and I our first bikes from JCPenney's for Christmas. The bikes were the best bikes JCPenney's had at that time in our minds.

I was the belle of the neighborhood with my new bike.

And living in Memphis, I did not have to wait for Spring to ride it.

When I moved to St. Louis, who orchestrated the move and came home to Memphis to move us during the worst ice storm in history? DUANE.

He drove through the state of Arkansas with one half of the trailer truck on the shoulder and the other half on the highway. Dani and I had no clue how dangerous the trip was, nor were we worried because our Big Brother was driving. What was there to worry about?

As I prepared to go away to college, my mom was freaking out because the baby wanted to leave and all the colleges I applied to were far, far away. Duane, being Duane, tried to bribe me with a new Volkswagen Beetle—cost, $1,995—to stay here with Mom and go to school. I could not drive, so it had no effect. Off I went to college. But my Big Brother had to come to Xavier and check on his little sister and drop big money in my little hands when he came.

A Big Brother who was "The King" in my eyes, he was the first Black Man I ever knew who learned how to believe it and conceive it, which meant he could achieve it.

To this day, he is the only person I know who owned an Excalibur car. What Black Man you know has the patience to wait a year for a car to be made? He did. If only for the joy of being the only Black Man in St. Louis with one, it was worth the wait.

He dreamed dreams others just read and marveled about. He found a way to bring his dreams, no matter how outlandish, to life. However short-lived that life was. My brother and I had our rocky times, more because his brand of humor and mine did not exist on the same planet, and also, children were to be seen and not heard according to him. And in his eyes, I was always a child. And in my lifetime being the youngest of a very large family, I was determined to be heard. (Smile.)

But all jokes aside, he was the one who had the biggest influence on me, instilling impossible dreams in my children and believing I could achieve impossible dreams for myself. I will miss you, Big Brother, even though your younger days were your better days. I rest, assured you now have found peace and are rocking and crying tears of joy in the Bosom of your mother, the one woman who never gave up on you and always had your back, right or wrong.

Love, Your baby sister, Spring

MY BEST MALE FRIEND

Who can you depend on to tell you the truth when your girlfriends are afraid to?

My best male friend.

Who can listen with the all-listening ear and tell you exactly what you want to hear, about how a man thinks, perceives our feminine perspective?

And have a rebuttal to each and every objection? Yet be there when I need him, with finance, not romance, huh? My best male friend.

Who is a man of few words and gets straight to the point?

Not take cross-country detours or belabor the point.

Not having any hesitation is necessary, you see. For my best male friend is all man and has the gift of honesty, loyalty, no gossiping about me.

He know just how a real friend should be. That's why he's my best male friend.

We can hang out and shoot the breeze. I can call him up whenever I please.

He doesn't hesitate to say to his fellows who are there, excuse me while I take this call, please.

For he can tell by the intonation and trembling in my voice, it's him I need to give me that old-time male perspective. To jolt me back into reality.

Not think less of me because of my need.

Yet know not to cross that boundary at that time for physical intimacy.

Hey, that's why you are my best male friend.

REFLECTIONS OF MAINTENANCE DETAIL

Days of waking up to fulfill a purpose to encourage children and keep them safe in a clean, healthy environment. That was my purpose.

Days of waking up with the sun and leaving work as the moon reached its apex just to make sure the boiler worked, the heat was on full blast, the trash cans were emptied, and, less not forget, the floors gleaming and the doors locked.

Days of waking up with the sun to throw out salt and shovel the parking lot so the educators, administrators and all school personnel and parents could access the school grounds safely during inclement weather.

Days of waking up with the sun and the only scent you smell is the smell of Bengay, which was absorbed in your pores from the night before due to moving furniture and boxes and supplies all day long.

Days of waking up with the sun and being the very first presence at the school to open the doors and turn on the lights and make sure the perimeter is safe before staff come in.

Days of waking up with the sun, hoping for a slow day, and all day long is filled with cleaning up after children's accidents and getting overstuffed objects out of the plumbing system and opening classrooms where teachers accidently locked their keys in the room and getting two and three back-to-back calls on the walkie-talkie stating this must be done NOW.

Days of waking up with the sun and dreaming all day of getting off at 2:30 p.m. and being told at 2:00 p.m., hey, we got a special program tomorrow morning in the gym. We need you to set up 300 chairs AND POSITION IN A SQUARE FOUR LONG TABLES FOR THE EVENT THAT STARTS AT 8 a.m. So could you do that before you leave for the day?

After several years of getting up with the sun and focusing on agendas and plans laid out by other men, God has decided that now is the time for retirement.

I no longer have to get up with the sun or work while glancing at the moonlight in an empty building, working to prepare it to receive hundreds of laughing, smiling, joyous faces that arrive there every day for school. Now I can contemplate if I want to wake up with the *Today Show* or wait until after Hoda and Kathie Lee. Or I can just sleep the day away, getting up whenever it suits my fancy.

Some will say they stayed as long as they did for the check. DO NOT BELIEVE THEM!!!

They stayed as long as I did because we felt we could make a difference in making the school environment a comfortable learning environment. And we stayed at it as long as we did because most of the time, we did not feel anyone else would care as much as we did. We wanted the job done right.

But now it is someone else's problem, not ours.

Retirement has definitely been earned, and a never-ending holiday is well deserved.

I know I will really relish my decision when the first snow falls and we have over 3 inches. And it's 5 degrees outside, and now I don't have to budge from my warm bed or get up to warm my car and leave home before the streets are plowed.

I'll be able to smile and change positions in my bed and drift back off to sleep, enjoying the real benefits of retirement—a never-ending snow day.

A tribute to school maintenance staff—hometown heroes

THE PRINCIPAL

P is for Patience, which you need each day.

R is for Responsibility, which constantly comes our way.

I is for Intellect, which you surely need an ample supply.

N is to let Nothing deter you from your task.

C is for Courage that's needed to stay steadfast.

I stands for integrity, which must be in abundant measure.

P is for Perseverance, to stick with God first.

A is for Academic, which must be the focal point.

L is for the leadership that you exhibit each day.

VILLAGE RAISED

Today, we the people of Hadiyah's village jointly and wonderfully praise GOD and acknowledge that through him, all blessings flow.

Today is a celebration of Hadiyah's village. The village of relatives, elders, mentors, acquaintances, professors, educators, mental health professionals, volunteers, participants in community endeavors, peers, best friends, colleagues, sorority sisters and just a few of us who have been blessed to breathe and exhale in the same air space as this vision of elegance and poise.

Who with a soft, gentle voice of determination has made so much noise on the national and international scene in the name of scientific research.

In the name of encouraging the youth of tomorrow to step out of their circumstance and dream the dreams that are perceived to be unattainable and pursue careers that are considered nontraditional or socioeconomically "not" the field that African Americans pursue.

Hadiyah, today your Counsel of Elders and your entire village salute you for never letting anything deter or anyone deter you from your GOD-given purpose in life. I speak for your village of elders whose life circumstances added fuel to your purpose and for them who are resting in the bosom of Abraham lobbying and interceding for you. They, too, want you to know, "JOB WELL DONE, JOB WELL DONE." For within your village, each one of us in our own small part of your glorious whole says, "Hail today to this child who was village raised and exemplifies the African proverb: 'IT TAKES A VILLAGE TO RAISE A CHILD.'"

A tribute to the magnanimous accomplishment of Dr. Hadiyah-Nicole Green receiving her PHD in Physics from University of Alabama–Birmingham

THE WOMAN WITHIN

Welcome, Woman of Strength.

Welcome, Woman with the All-seeing Eye.

The woman who corrects her child just before that child puts a negative thought into action,

Which leaves child to believe mother really does have eyes in the back of her head.

Welcome, Woman of Endurance. You who has endured a thousand moments challenging and rejecting your worth; a thousand perceptions that your beauty is not fitting the scale or making the grade.

Welcome, Woman who chose not to allow the naysayers within your midst to define you or discourage you.

Truly you have been knocked down, bruised and beaten.

But never have they defeated you.

You have arisen like the phoenix glistening on the horizon.

You have exhibited fortitude of spirit, for the whole world to see.

For the world to marvel at your willpower and perseverance that propels you to the top of every situation.

Woman Within, Woman who is strong enough to hold us, nurture us in her womb. Strong enough to work a 9-to-5 job and still come home and work from 6 to 10.

Woman, I am amazed at your courage, determination and moral fiber within you that holds it all together.

Thank God for that Woman Within You.

SOMEWHERE OVER THE HORIZON

Somewhere over the horizon is the answer to all our problems.

Somewhere over the horizon is a place of peace and tranquility.

Somewhere out there, women are beautiful, vibrant human beings. Women who are respected for their gifts of maintaining and sustaining normalcy and healthy environments for their families.

Somewhere out there, women are championed because they can take a meal meant for four and stretch it so six go to bed full.

Somewhere out there, women contribute to the professional workplace without compromising their womanness or values.

Somewhere out there are men who can accept constructive criticism with a smile from a female.

Somewhere out there, men know that sensitivity, compassion and the display of feelings through tearful outbursts occasionally add an intimate kind of genuineness to her demeanor.

Somewhere out there, the small things we do for each other without thought of a reward or commendation are seen as rewarding, life-sustaining experiences.

Somewhere out there, commitment and increased focus of one's partner's desires, needs and capabilities are a given in a relationship for the man and woman.

Somewhere out there over the horizon, man and woman have learned how to respect and check each other without negativity, and two have finally learned to operate as one.

WALKING IN DELIVERANCE

Walking into deliverance, that is sure to come.

Thanking you in advance for the healing of my mind, body and soul.

Thanking you for keeping me and never leaving me during the midnight hours when my faith became weak.

Walking into a deliverance that is sure to come.

Deliverance from lack of…in a sea of abundance.

Deliverance from a mindset of pity and apathy.

Deliverance from being unemployed, to being employed and fulfilled.

Deliverance from waking up with dreams and no road map of execution.

Deliverance from the fake smile of "it's a great day" when your soul is pained for feeling trapped in a standstill, "I'm going nowhere" moment.

God, thank you for a roof over my head, clothes on my back and transportation to and fro.

Thank you for food to be full and a healthy body as I await this storm to pass.

Deliverance from the warring factions warring for my soul because Jesus has taken a hold of me.

SOMEWHERE 'YOU' ARE THERE

When I close my eyes and fantasize about my most
vivid memories,

Of being and feeling like a complete, totally desirable
woman, who is loved, cherished, respected and adored,
Somewhere You Are There.

When my back is up against the wall and my confidence
is shattered and I feel like I can't go on, I hear your
voice shouting out in the wilderness of my existence,
"You got this, baby."

I know Somewhere You Are There being my number
one cheerleader.

When I finally accomplish an arduous task and
tears of triumph spring from my eyes, and the
audience of naysayers ask, how did you do it?
Who in GOD's name helped you to
accomplish the impossible?

I Know Somewhere You Were There and are there
now and forever more. You are my first thought
as I welcome into a new day.

And my last thought as I prepare to rest to meet the
next one.

Even though I can't see you, or touch you, I Know,
GOD, that Somewhere You Are There.

Notes of Jazz

When I was a kid I hated Jazz because my parents only allowed us to listen to it on Sundays - no other music was allowed. During a stressful, angry moment in my life, I turned on my car radio and it landed on a Jazz station. The savage beast of road rage dissipated and the harmonious soothing sounds of the instruments calmed me and took me out of my stress. That was my first experience realizing that Jazz could transform.

To me, Jazz is the healing balm to the Blues. Because to live in this world we must have challenges and trials to make us stronger and help elevate our understanding of faith.

Jazz can be a blend of hearing a sad message like Nancy Wilson's song "Guess Who I Saw Today," with melodious vocal chords and clap back fused with the band's unique delivery of notes. So though she goes from believing she's in a committed relationship to finding out her partner is sharing his goodness with another woman, by the end of the song, everyone is smiling at the end of the song.

Jazz soothes. Like the Gospel song lyrics "My soul looks back and wonders how I got over," the poem *Jazz Is My Life* was written as a tribute to a very close friend who began a Jazz Foundation. He has spent over 40 years recording interviews with Jazz Masters and teaching others the importance of preserving musical history

JAZZ IS MY LIFE

When the trials of life bring me a boatload of strife, I reach for Lena, Billie, Chico, Miles, Lionel, Basie and such.

I reach for them because their soulful chords and bebop hues melt away the stress and help me to realize how blessed I am to have this sweet, sweet, sweet release...

Jazz is my life.

Every 411 moment, thoughts consume me of how to reach the masses about this wonderful Black experience that has gone global, virtual and now knows no ethnic limitation.

Jazz is my life.

And with every breath I take, I will promote it. I will embrace the healing flow of the melodious chords that make heavenly music with the blending of drums, sax, bass, trumpet and flute, not to mention alto, tenor, and soprano. Boy, just thinking of the versatile collaborations is too much.

Jazz is my life.

If you don't understand that, that is your life, not mine.

I'm doing fine and feel empowered on this journey to a dream fulfilled. Come join the ride if you understand.

BILLY STRAYHORN

Billy Strayhorn, shy, gifted pianist, classically trained.

Billy Strayhorn composed and arranged music that made it easy to listen to and go to sleep.

It also pumped up your adrenaline if you needed to creep. To top it off, his music was soothing enough to calm the savage beast.

The up-tempo beat of Strayhorn's rendition of RAIN CHECK made me check my worries at the door and totally become absorbed in the melodies as the music caressed me and possessed me.

Listening to LUSH LIFE's pure distinct sound makes you want to lie around and let the music serenade you all night long.

His professional marriage to "The Duke" spanned three decades. Their union was so productive, it revolutionized collaborative musical genius.

Billy Strayhorn did not seek the spotlight. But his gift made it impossible for him to avoid it.

A Flower Is a Lovesome Thing, Johnny Come Lately, Lotus Blossom, Clementine, Day Dream, Multicolored Blue, A Drum Is a Woman, all were compositions that were a testament of Something to Live For.

And Billy, your music was something to die for.

COUNT BASIE

Thank you, Count Basie, for your majestic Big Band sound.

Thank you for nurturing all those unique voices that you promoted.

Lady Day, Ella, Joe Williams and Jimmy Rushing are but a few.

You could play the piano, organ and sometimes drums.

Talk about a one-man band; you had it going on.

And to top it all off, your personality and smile were second to none.

Composer, bandleader, musician, lover of blues, jazz and swing; you traveled to the Midwest, Kansas City and the World, doing your thing.

You became a Jazz Master in 1982; even made the Hollywood Walk of Fame in the 1970s.

We loved you for your generous spirit and, most of all, for your creativity.

Count, I'm most thankful I got to see you during those last years you were here on Earth.

Your hard work and dedication to your craft were a statement to your worth.

DINAH WASHINGTON

Dinah, labeled Queen of the Blues.

Dinah mastered jazz, blues and R&B.

Dinah, how awesome you became.

You even sang before queens and claimed you out-reigned them.

Dinah, only your sex appeal matched your zeal for life and adventure.

Dinah, we wish you were still here crooning in the clubs and making your transition from LPs to CDs and disk.

Dinah, you only lived 39 years yet were inducted in the Big Band and Jazz Hall of Fame.

Dinah, you and Quincy Jones made some beautiful music together. Dinah, the true you, we hardly knew.

You were so complex for the time frame of which you reigned supreme.

Dinah Washington, your vocals are still soothing the savage beast.

Dinah, thank you for blessing us with your masterful jazzy vocals that remind us of the range and depth of your vocal intensity.

Dinah, you were one bad mother for ya!

DIONNE

Dionne, Dionne, such a gifted voice of style and grace.

Singing for the Lord since age 6, what a testament of faith that makes. Singing such songs as Yes, Jesus Loves Me and I Say a Little Prayer...she also sang Pop and R&B, What a musician extraordinaire.

In her lifetime, Dionne has been a singer, producer, commentator, activist, actress and, most important role yet, mother of two. She is the poster child for if you can believe it, you can achieve it.

She began in church singing with family who are Legends of Gospel Music. Unlike most African American artists of her time, she did not begin on the Chitlin' Circuit.

Dionne mesmerized Burt Bacharach and Hal David and was their muse of songwriting inspiration for many a year. Do You Know the Way to San Jose, Message to Michael, Anyone Who Had a Heart set her vocals apart from the rest, wooing primarily white audiences initially who would pay dearly to be entertained by Dionne. She was one of the first Afro-American crossover artists of her time. The changing musical climates of the times put her to the test to see if she could remain a thriving force after her style and type of musical delivery were no longer at the forefront of Billboard's top hit parade.

But Dionne is a survivor first and a business woman second. She just changed gears and hosted Solid Gold and too many other variety shows to be told and kept on keeping on.

She did several duets with male and female musical greats, such as The Man & Woman Tour with Isaac Hayes and the Super Women Tour with Legendary Patti LaBelle and Gladys Knight. She was an International Ambassador who became world renowned for her humanitarian efforts.

Dionne, only you were able to master the art of keeping your private life private and raising your children without them being under the umbrella of media scrutiny. The average person hardly knows the real you.

But Oprah labeled you a Female Legend of our time and honored you as such. Dionne, Dionne, we love the beautiful music you make so much. Dionne, how great now is your fame. Just saying your first name Dionne, makes people know there is only one Dionne, and Dionne Warwick is her name.

THE DUKE

The Duke, The Duke, none can compare to his handsome, debonair flair for life, love and the ability to entertain, explain, compose and play the hell out of the Piano.

The Piano and Duke were one being, not two separate entities.

The Duke, no matter the life crisis, his talent could not be disputed.

No matter the new style or genre of music, the Duke's elaborate talent and Big Band Ensemble reigned head and shoulders above the rest.

You just can't shortcut perfection. He was skilled as a composer, arranger, conductor and author of too many scores to mention.

He and Billy Strayhorn collaborated on so many masterpieces, the entire music world paid attention. We will forever remember Take the "A" Train, Sophisticated Lady, Mood Indigo and It Don't Mean a Thing (If It Ain't Got That Swing).

He was internationally known though Washington D.C. is where he was born.

The Duke is in the Grammy Hall of Fame and received awards, tributes and memorials too numerous to name.

His last words were a summation of himself:

"Music is how I live, why I live and how I will be remembered."

For *Music Is My Mistress*.

THE FIRST LADY OF SONG

Lady Ella, as she was known, could sing in a vocal range spanning three octaves.

Ella's voice tone was so pure as to be classified as perfection.

Nobody could improvise and scat like Lady Ella.

Ella was so bad she had her own Orchestra.

Her signature song, which everyone knew her by, was her 1938 hit A-Tisket, A-Tasket.

Ella was the most popular female Jazz performer for over 50 years.

She was known the world over as the Scat Queen. She sold over 40 million albums.

Ella was a woman entrepreneur and businesswoman.

Even though she died at age 79, she left a multitude of vocal tracks for us to relax and sit back and groove off of her harmonious intonations and scatty expressions she comprised in over 59 years in show business.

Lady Ella, you are truly the First Lady of Song, and I don't know how we will get along without you.

HAZEL SCOTT

Hazel Scott, a black female musical genius that time forgot.

Hazel, a mixture of Caribbean spice and American pizzazz.

Boy, what you were able to accomplish with your classical piano skill and all that Jazz...puts you in a class all by yourself.

The way you made the piano talk as your hands moved over the keys in a movement that resembled a high-speed chase could not erase to all who were listening that it was truly a heavenly experience.

A child prodigy, Julliard schooled. So talented, you were accepted at age 8 and privately trained. You overcame prejudice and racial barriers at such an early age. The whole world was truly your stage.

You broke racial stereotypes in film and in musical arenas too. Demanding financial and artistic parity while singing with flawless clarity. You had contracts that insisted your audiences included both black and white patrons.

Hazel canceled her show if the promoters acted like they did not understand.

Hazel Scott, an original Black Beauty.

Such a pity that racial temerity and communist hysteria caused you to seek European opportunities.

I wonder how many African Americans had to flee our shores just to have the right to be all GOD commissioned them to be.

This is the real American tragedy.

Hazel Scott, you were truly the 8th wonder of the world, mastering seven languages and singing in perfect pitch. You go, girl.

Your renditions of Takin' a Chance and Rhapsody in Blue only showed a fraction of your creative genius to me.

Married to Adam Clayton Powell Jr., what a "Wow" couple you two turned out to be.

You two represented power, equality and charismatic virtuosity.

Hazel, even though prejudice, jealousy and bigotry have clouded the awareness of your greatness in African American history, your time has finally come where the world will now see all the extraordinary accomplishments you made in such a brief time span during your lifetime.

Pioneering with your own radio show, TV show and film appearances too. Most of the time being cast to play You.

All the while doing this at a time when segregation and black hostility reigned supreme.

Hazel Scott truly mastered the American Dream.

LADY DAY

Billie Holiday was her name.

A tormented genius, slightly ahead of her time.

Singing ballads that raised the consciousness

Of the people regarding the Black man's plight.

My personal favorite, Strange Fruit.

She sang of the Klu Klux Klan's ritual of capturing Black men under the cloak of darkness and hanging them from trees with such regularity as you would pick fruit from a tree.

Her tormented childhood and incidents of racial discrimination gave her an intense ability to capture and portray the pain and agony of her people.

Her presence of singing with a beautiful fresh white gardenia in her hair set you up for the moving, heart-stirring emotions you felt while listening to her sing bluesy tunes of woe, pain, heartache and suffering.

Lady Day, as she was called, succumbed to the call of addiction to ease the pain and suffering of being misjudged and mistreated just because she was born Black. The one thing about herself she could not change.

Lady Day, your moving ballads are a testament to your greatness. And God Bless the Child is a testament to your musical genius and skill. Lady Day, you were truly born too soon.

NANCY WILSON

Nancy, Nancy, Nancy, what can I say? I was only 16 years old when I first heard "Guess Who I Saw Today."

The words mesmerized me and touched deep, deep, deep within my soul. The clever way you checked your man made me admire the way you made him feel like dung, yet it was spoken with style, grace and finesse, and not a cuss word was uttered.

Nancy, Nancy, Nancy, over 50 years of entertaining us and making us forget our cares and troubles while you captivated us under your spell for a little while.

Nancy, I don't know if you know how many men, women and teens grew up listening to the way you wove singing into an art of storytelling.

Nancy, Nancy, Nancy, you are truly a female Jazz Master. Thank God for you and your musical legacy.

Q

Some people when they hear the word "Thriller," it conjures up visions of Michael Jackson. But when I hear the word "Thriller," I envision all of the Thrills you have given the world through the vast musical genres you have become master of: Jazz, Swing, Big Band, R&B, Pop, Rock, Hip-Hop. Man, is there an area of music you haven't conquered?

Everybody who is anybody in music in the 20th century, you knew or worked with. You have been a record composer, film composer, television and record producer, musical arranger, conductor, and let's not forget, you are a musician. Your career has spanned seven decades.

Who else can say they have 79 Grammy Award nominations?

Q, you are a legend on so many levels.

I know watching your childhood and young adult playmates transition to the great beyond has to be one of the great setbacks to living a long life.

But what I admire the most about you, Q, is you keep on challenging yourself to forge into new frontiers. And this is after the rest of us thought you had already conquered all that could be conquered.

Q, not many people can survive brain surgery and still continue to produce work that is considered more a work of art than the masterpieces you created before undergoing the knife.

I appreciate you, Q, for how you have conquered all the struggles and challenges in your life: lies, wives, afflictions, bad business plans and, hardest of all, seeing your friends succumb to addictions. Yet you are still standing.

Q, you are more than a Musical Phenomenon.

Q, you are second to none.

THELONIUS MONK

Mr. Straight, No Chaser, founder of Bebop.

He was a straight shooter and loyal too. If you were friend of Monk's, you were a friend for life.

His composition of Pannonica is such a light, delicate piece that speaks of harmony, peace and reminds you of the experience of being seduced by a very patient and skilled lover. A lover who takes his time to hit all the right spots like he has a whole lifetime to make love to you instead of a few moments…

Thelonius, Thelonious, when your hands touched the piano, you created masterpieces few could duplicate or anticipate, and try as they might, their brain could not capture your brain waves' flight plan to transcribe what notes their ears had heard.

Thelonius, Thelonius, your personal life, though filled with strive as everyone tried to pigeonhole you into some preconceived category that did not exist, your flair for fashion and topping your head with a hat for whatever occasion made you the prototype for the original Beatnik persona.

All this helped make your genius more than legendary. Not to mention your patron, who was of British royal blood, who forsook the life she knew to follow you.

Unfortunately, one of the drawbacks of musically creating and giving your all constantly and getting little back made you get off track.

The beginnings of self-doubt began to eat at the core of your soul. This made you, we are told, begin to exhibit moments of loss of control of your emotional and mental stability.

Through your vast musical compositions, we now are able to still listen and witness your true mastery of the arts at work.

ABOUT THE AUTHOR

Spignotta Milam, a woman of many lifetimes and experiences.

Professionally, Spignotta has been a Licensed Clinical Social Worker for over 30 years. She has held numerous job titles such as assistant director of a homeless shelter; school social worker; individual, group, family and couple psychotherapist; substance abuse clinician; substitute teacher; storyteller and poet.

Spignotta has served on the board of a community center and is an active member of her sorority, Delta Sigma Theta. She also was a contributor of several scholarship initiatives with her sorority and Tennessee State University.

Spignotta is the mother of three phenomenally gifted adult children: two daughters and one son. She loves to travel, read, listen to live music and is actively involved with her church's children's ministry.